LONDON COLLEGE OF MUSIC

C000116566

Step One

Classical Guitar Playing

Compiled by
Tony Skinner, Raymond Burley and Amanda Cook
on behalf of

The Specialists in Guitar Education

RGT®

Registry of Guitar Tutors

Printed and bound in Great Britain

A CIP record for this publication is available from the British Library
ISBN: 978-1-905908-19-6

Published by Registry Publications

Registry Mews, Wilton Rd, Bexhill, Sussex, TN40 1HY

Cover artwork by Danielle Croft. Design by JAK Images.

Compiled for LCM Exams by

www.RGT.org

INTRODUCTION

This publication is part of a progressive series of ten handbooks, primarily intended for candidates considering taking the London College Of Music examinations in classical guitar playing. However, given each handbook's wide content of musical repertoire and associated educational material, the series provides a solid foundation of musical education for any classical guitar student – whether intending to take an examination or not. Whilst the handbooks can be used for independent study, they are ideally intended as a supplement to individual or group tuition.

Examination entry

An examination entry form is provided at the rear of each handbook. This is the only valid entry form for the London College Of Music classical guitar examinations.

Please note that *if the entry form is detached and lost, it will not be replaced under any circumstances* and the candidate will be required to obtain a replacement handbook to obtain another entry form.

Editorial information

Examination performances must be from this handbook edition. All performance pieces should be played in full, including all repeats shown; the pieces have been edited specifically for examination use, with all non-required repeat markings omitted.

Tempos, fingering and dynamic markings are for general guidance only and need not be rigidly adhered to, providing an effective musical result is achieved.

Pick-hand fingering is normally shown on the stem side of the notes:
p = thumb; *i* = index finger; *m* = middle finger; *a* = third finger.

Fret-hand fingering is shown with the numbers **1 2 3 4**, normally to the left of the notehead.
0 indicates an open string.

String numbers are shown in a circle, normally below the note. For example, ⑥ = 6th string.

Dynamic markings are written under the staves. Some of the following may be used:
p = play softly;   *f* = play strongly;   *mp* = moderately soft;   *mf* = moderately strong.

TECHNICAL WORK

andidates should play the scales shown below *from memory*. Scales should be played ascending and descending, i.e. from the lowest note to the highest note and back again, without a pause and without repeating the top note.

Suggested fret-hand fingering is provided with the notation below, and it is recommended that scales are picked using alternating *i* and *m* fingering. However, to allow for flexibility in teaching approaches, the fingering suggestions are not compulsory and alternative systematic fingerings that are musically effective will be accepted. Either tirando (free stroke) or apoyando (rest stroke) can be used.

At this level, scales should be played at an appropriate tempo of 104 beats per minute. Slightly slower or faster performances will be acceptable, providing that the tempo is maintained evenly throughout.

Overall, the examiner will be listening for accurate, even and clear playing.

A maximum of 25 marks may be awarded in this section of the examination.

C major scale – 1 octave

A harmonic minor scale – 1 octave

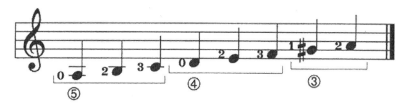

PERFORMANCE _____

Candidates should play any two melodies from Group A, plus any one piece from Group B. A maximum of 60 marks may be awarded in this section of the examination – i.e. up to 20 marks for each performance. Tempo markings are for general guidance only and do not need to be adhered to strictly. All repeat markings should be followed.

Performance Tips

Melodies:

- *Hungarian Dance* by Brahms is in the key of A minor; the other melodies are all in the key of C major. This means that the notes contained in the melodies will be taken from either the A minor or C major scales, which are shown in the Technical Work section of this handbook – so it would be helpful preparation to study these scales first.

- Occasionally the melodies will include notes that, whilst still within the key, are just beyond the one octave scale.

- Hungarian Dance features a *first and second-time ending*: at the end of bar 16 the piece should be repeated from the beginning; on the repeat playing, bar 16 should be omitted and replaced with the two bars in the second-time ending.

Elegy:

- The melody lies in the bass and should be played throughout with the thumb. The repeated open high E string is there just to give a sense of movement and contrast; it should not be played too loudly.

- The title *Elegy* suggests a mournful or reflective character to the piece.

- The first 8 bars should be repeated before progressing to bar 9.

Ritmico:

- This piece involves a repeated *a m i* right-hand finger pattern in many bars, but be careful with the timing where this pattern changes. Aim for a lively and steady tempo to capture the rhythmical feel of the piece.

- Begin with a strong tone, but take note of the changes in dynamics.

- Once all 12 bars have been played, the whole piece should be repeated from the beginning.

Kindness:

- This Russian melody is in the key of A minor. The tune is accompanied by two open string bass notes per bar.

- After bar 8 the first six bars are repeated; the last two bars of each eight-bar section should be played more softly than the preceding six bars.

- Notice the distinctive two-bar rhythm (1&2 3&4, 1 2 3_) that is repeated throughout the entire piece.

Sunbeams On The Sea:

- The first three bars of this piece consist of a repeated alternation between the open first and third strings, while a slow descending bassline occurs on the fifth string. There is no melody as such, instead the treble and bass parts combine to create an impressionistic effect.

- Notice how the first three bars are repeated on two occasions later on in the piece.

- Observe the change in dynamic that occurs at bar 10; playing more softly here will help to enhance the harmonic change that takes place.

Jesu, Joy of Man's Desiring

Johann Sebastian Bach
(1685 – 1750)

[Group A]

Carnival of Venice

Julius Benedict
(1804 – 1885)

[Group A]

6

Hungarian Dance No. 4

[Group A]

Johannes Brahms
(1833 – 1897)

The Skaters

[Group A]

Emil Waldteufel
(1837 – 1915)

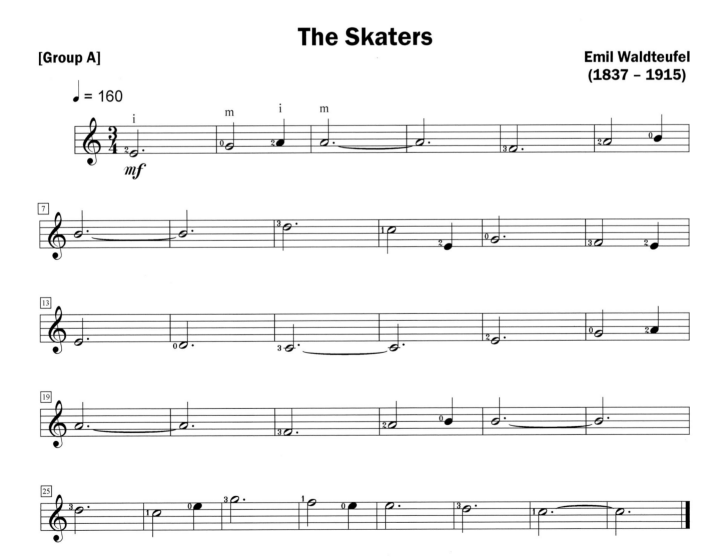

Elegy

[Group B]

Lawrence Sabor
(1950 – 2001)

Ritmico

[Group B]

Franz Biederman
(1958 –)

8

Kindness

[Group B]

Oleg Kiselev
(1964 –)

Sunbeams On The Sea

[Group B]

Amanda Cook
(1976 –)

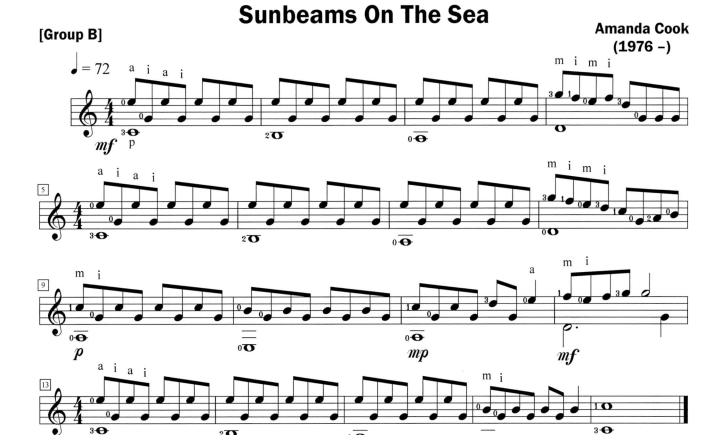

VIVA VOCE

The examiner will ask questions, based on the music performed, to test the candidate's knowledge of the stave, bar lines, notes and rests. The information below provides a summary of what is required.

A maximum of 15 marks may be awarded in this section of the examination.

The stave

The notes on the lines (E G B D F) can be remembered by making up an unusual phrase such as:
Enormous **G**uitarists **B**reak **D**ainty **F**ootstools
The notes in the spaces between the lines form the word **FACE**.

Bar lines

A bar is a way of dividing music into manageable portions. It makes music easier to read and makes it easier to discover where the main beat lies. The end of each bar is indicated by a vertical line called a *bar line*. The space between each pair of bar lines, where the notes are written, is called a bar (also known as a *measure*). At the end of the last bar, or a section, of a piece of music there are two vertical lines. These are called a *double bar line*.

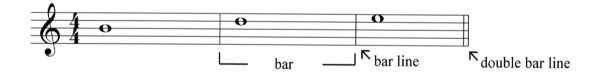

Notes and rests

The table below shows the names of the notes and rests, and their values. (You can use either the traditional or modern terminology when identifying notes).

Traditional name	Modern name	Note	Rest	Value in crotchet beats
semibreve	whole note	o	▬	4
dotted minim	dotted half note	𝅗𝅥.	▬.	3
minim	half note	𝅗𝅥	▬	2
crotchet	quarter note	♩	𝄽	1
quaver	eighth note	♪	𝄾	½

Classical Guitar
Examination Entry Form
STEP ONE

The standard LCM Exams music entry form is NOT valid for Classical Guitar entries.
Entry to the examination is only possible via this original form.
Photocopies of this form will not be accepted under any circumstances.

Please use black ink and block capital letters when completing this form.

SESSION (Spring/Summer/Winter): _____ YEAR: _____

Preferred Examination Centre (if known): _____
If left blank you will be examined at the nearest venue to your home address.

Candidate Details:

Candidate Name (as to appear on certificate):

_____

Candidate ID (if entered previously): _____ Date of birth: _____

Gender (M/F): _____ Ethnicity (see chart overleaf): _____

Date of birth and ethnicity details are for statistical purposes only, and are not passed on to the examiner.

☐ Tick this box if you are attaching details of particular needs requirements.

Teacher Details:

Teacher Name (as to appear on certificate): _____

Teacher Qualifications (if required on certificate): _____

LCM Teacher Code (if entered previously): _____

Address: _____

_____ Postcode: _____

Tel. No. (day): _____ (evening): _____

☐ Tick this box if any details above have changed since your last LCM entry.

IMPORTANT NOTES

- It is the candidate's responsibility to have knowledge of, and comply with, the current syllabus requirements. Where candidates are entered for examinations by a teacher, the teacher must take responsibility that candidates are entered in accordance with the current syllabus requirements. Failure to carry out any of the examination requirements may lead to disqualification.

- For candidates with particular needs, a letter giving details and requests for any special requirements (e.g. enlarged sight reading), together with an official supporting document (e.g. medical certificate), should be attached.

- Examinations may be held on any day of the week, including weekends. Any appointment requests (e.g. 'prefer morning,' or 'prefer weekdays') must be made at the time of entry. **LCM Exams and its Representatives will take note of the information given; however, no guarantees can be made that all wishes can be met.**

- Submission of this entry is an undertaking to abide by the current regulations.

ETHNIC ORIGIN CLASSIFICATIONS

White
01   British
02   Irish
03   Other white background

Mixed
04   White and black Caribbean
05   White and black African
06   White and Asian
07   Other mixed background

Asian or Asian British
08   Indian
09   Pakistani
10   Bangladeshi
11   Other Asian background

Black or Black British
12   Caribbean
13   African
14   Other black background

Chinese or Other Ethnic Group
15   Chinese
16   Other

17   **Prefer not to say**

Examination Fee: £ _____

Late Entry Fee (if necessary)   £ _____

Total amount submitted: £ _____

Cheques or postal orders should be made payable to '*University of West London*'.

A list of current fees, entry deadlines and session dates is available from LCM Exams.

Where to submit your entry form

Entries for public centres should be sent to the
**LCM Exams local examination centre representative
(NOT to the LCM Exams Head Office).**

View the LCM Exams website www.uwl.ac.uk/lcmexams
or contact the LCM Exams office (tel: 020 8231 2364 / email: lcm.exams@uwl.ac.uk)
for details of your nearest local examination centre representative.

Entries for the London area only, or for private centres, should be sent direct to:
LCM Exams, University of West London, Walpole House, 18-22 Bond St, London, W5 5AA

Official Entry Form